Cooking
step-by-step

THIS EDITION
Senior Editor Carrie Love
Assistant Editor Syed Tuba Javed
US Senior Editor Shannon Beatty
US Editor Margaret Parrish
US Culinary Consultant Renee Wilmeth
Senior Art Editors Rachael Parfitt Hunt, Kanika Kalra
Art Editor Mohd Zishan
Publishing Assistant Anna Bonnerjea
Jacket Designer Rachael Parfitt Hunt
Photographer Ruth Jenkinson
Home Economist and Food Stylist Denise Smart
Recipe Tester Charlotte Simpkins
Assistant Picture Research Administrator Manpreet Kaur
DTP Designers Dheeraj Singh, Syed Md Farhan
Managing Editors Penny Smith, Monica Saigal
Managing Art Editor Ivy Sengupta
Production Editor Becky Fallowfield
Senior Production Controller Ben Radley
Delhi Creative Head Malavika Talukder
Publisher Francesca Young
Art Director Mabel Chan
Managing Director Sarah Larter

PREVIOUS EDITION
Senior Editor James Mitchem
Senior Designer Elaine Hewson
US Senior Editor Shannon Beatty
US Editor Christy Lusiak
US Recipe Consultant Kate Ramos
Designers Charlotte Bull, Samantha Richiardi
Editorial Assistance Sally Beets, Carrie Love
Art Direction for Photography Charlotte Bull
Photographer Dave King
Home Economist and Food Stylist Denise Smart
Recipe Tester Sue Davie
Pre-production Producer Tony Phipps
Senior Producer John Casey
Jacket Designer Charlotte Bull
Jacket Coordinator Francesca Young
Creative Technical Support Sonia Charbonnier
Managing Editor Penny Smith
Managing Art Editor Mabel Chan
Publisher Mary Ling
Art Director Jane Bull

This American Edition, 2024
First American Edition, 2018
Published in the United States by DK Publishing,
a division of Penguin Random House LLC
1745 Broadway, 20th Floor, New York, NY 10019

Copyright © 2018, 2024 Dorling Kindersley Limited
24 25 26 27 28 10 9 8 7 6 5 4 3 2 1
001–340990–Sep/2024

A catalog record for this book
is available from the Library of Congress.
ISBN 978-0-5938-4359-8

DK books are available at special discounts when purchased
in bulk for sales promotions, premiums, fund-raising,
or educational use.
For details, contact: DK Publishing Special Markets,
1745 Broadway, 20th Floor, New York, NY 10019
SpecialSales@dk.com

Printed and bound in China

www.dk.com

MIX
Paper | Supporting
responsible forestry
FSC™ C018179

This book was made with Forest
Stewardship Council™ certified
paper—one small step in DK's
commitment to a sustainable future.
Learn more at
www.dk.com/uk/information/sustainability

Contents

Kitchen rules

Even the most experienced cooks need to follow kitchen rules. So, whether you're new to cooking or not, be sure to follow these guidelines so everyone is safe, healthy, and ready to have fun.

Hygiene

Being clean and careful in the kitchen will prevent germs from spreading and keep you from getting sick.

- Always wash your hands before you begin cooking, and wash them again if they get messy or if you touch raw meat, fish, or poultry.

- Use hot soapy water to clean cutting boards and knives used to cut raw meat, fish, or poultry.

- Be sure to check use-by dates on ingredients.

- All fruits and vegetables should be washed before you begin cooking with them.

- Tasting as you cook is part of the fun, but never try something containing uncooked meat, fish, poultry, or eggs.

Safety

Cooking is a lot of fun, but it can also be dangerous. Follow these steps to make sure you don't hurt yourself.

• Always have an adult around while you cook so they can watch out for you and help with the trickier or more dangerous steps of a recipe.

• Ask an adult to help whenever you need to touch anything hot; when you cut, peel, or grate an ingredient; or when you use a power appliance, such as a blender, oven, or microwave.

• Clean as you go and be sure to wipe up any spills.

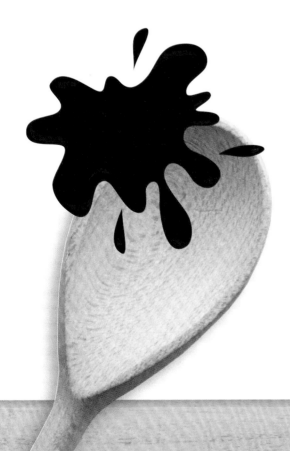

THIS SYMBOL MEANS YOU NEED TO ASK AN ADULT FOR HELP BECAUSE THE INSTRUCTIONS INVOLVE SOMETHING SHARP OR HOT.

Getting started

In this book, you'll find lots of simple, delicious, and fun recipes to make. But before you get started, take a few minutes to read about how best to prepare.

Before you start cooking

• Read each recipe all the way through before you begin; you don't want to get halfway through and realize you've forgotten a key ingredient.

• Gather all the equipment and ingredients together.

• Tie back long hair, roll up sleeves, and put an apron on.

Look out for these symbols:

Serves
How many people the dish serves, or how many portions it makes.

Preparation
How long the preparation takes (includes chilling, freezing, and marinating).

5 mins   30 mins   Serves 4

Cooking
How long the meal takes to cook.

These times are just guides, so use your judgment if you think a dish needs more time in the oven.

US standard measurements

oz = ounce
lb = pound
fl oz = fluid ounce

Weights and measurements

You'll find the ingredients you need for every dish clearly listed in each recipe. Measure them out before you begin. Here's a guide to what the abbreviations stand for.

Spoon measurements

tsp = teaspoon
tbsp = tablespoon

Tip:
If you get stuck when following a recipe or aren't sure what a word means, flip to the back of this book to find a handy glossary of kitchen terms.

Metric measurements

g = gram
ml = milliliter

Other important things you need to know

Seasoning

If a recipe suggests adding seasoning, this means you can add salt and/or pepper. Use just a little at a time so you don't put in too much.

Using the oven

An adult should always preheat your oven. This needs to be done for at least 15 minutes before using it so that it reaches the recommended temperature. Also, remember that cooking times can vary depending on the oven or pan you are using.

Vegetarian dishes

Look for this symbol on the contents page to find recipes suitable for vegetarians.

Variations

Some recipes in this book include suggested alternate options to the basic recipe, but don't be afraid to think of your own versions, too!

Equipment

Here's a list of equipment you'll need to make the recipes in this book. Before you cook a dish, read the recipe and assemble what you need.

Serving and dipping bowls

Heatproof bowl

Mixing bowl

Scales

Liquid measuring cup

Measuring cups

Plastic container

Salt and pepper grinders

Chopsticks

Cake slice

Honey drizzler

Wooden spoon

Serving spoon

Pastry brush

Paring knife

Knife

Fork

Tablespoon

Measuring spoons

Ladle

Garlic press

Frying pans

Grill pan

Small saucepan (with lid)

Large saucepan (with lid)

Wok

Saucepans

Parchment paper

Plastic wrap

Foil

Paper towels

Bamboo mat

Hand mixer

Colander

Microwave

The brownies on page 132 need to be cooked in a microwave.

Immersion blender

Food processor

Blender

Peeler

Pizza cutter

Can opener

Grater

Potato masher

Skewers

Strainers

Spatula

Whisk

Rolling pin

Tongs

Muffin liners

Cutting board

Muffin pan

Roasting pan

Cooling rack

Baking beans

Baking pan

Quiche pan

Ovenproof dish

Baking sheet

Cake pans

11

Light bites

These tempting recipes are
a mix of quick, simple snacks,
or dishes that are perfect for
sharing with your friends.

Ingredients

1lb 2oz (500g)
mixed berries
+
6 tbsp
sugar
+
1 tsp pure
vanilla extract
+
⅔ cup milk
+

Fluffy pancakes

Pancakes are the ultimate breakfast treat, especially with this berry compote. If you're short on time, just use regular fruit and top with yogurt, honey, or maple syrup.

GOOEY
FRUIT

MAKE
A STACK!

15 mins   10 mins   Makes 8–10

14

1 egg,
lightly beaten

2 tbsp
melted butter

¾ cup all-purpose
flour

1 tsp
baking powder

1 tbsp
sunflower oil

1

Stir gently to
dissolve the sugar.

Place the berries, 2 tbsp sugar, and
vanilla extract in a pan and bring to
a boil. Ask an adult to simmer the
mixture for 3–5 minutes and set aside.

2

Wet

Dry

Whisk the milk, egg, and butter in a liquid
measuring cup. Sift the flour, 4 tbsp sugar,
baking powder, and a pinch of salt into a
bowl. Beat the wet ingredients into the dry.

3

Watch for the bubbles!

Ask an adult to heat a nonstick pan over
medium heat. Add a little oil to the pan
and spoon in 2 tbsp of the mixture per
pancake. Cook for 2–3 minutes.

4

Add a little oil to
the pan between
batches to
prevent sticking.

Once bubbles appear, carefully flip
the pancakes and cook for another
2 minutes. Keep the pancakes warm
in the oven while you make the rest.

Omelets

A perfect omelet should be creamy, not rubbery. To achieve this texture, cook the omelet over low heat.

Ingredients

2 large eggs + ½ tsp butter

1

Break the eggs into a small bowl. Season with salt and freshly ground black pepper, then whisk together with a fork.

Variations

One of the best things about omelets is that they're easy to adapt. By adding these extra ingredients before folding, you can make several variations.

Cheese

Mushroom

2 tbsp Cheddar or Gruyère cheese

4 button mushrooms, chopped, cooked, and seasoned

2

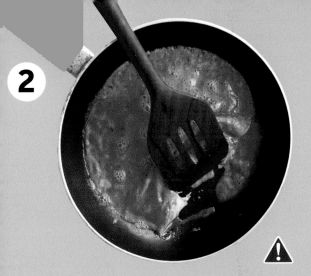

Ask an adult to heat the butter in a nonstick pan until foamy. Add the beaten eggs and swirl with a spatula. Carefully tilt the pan to let the egg run into any gaps.

3

Continue cooking for 30 seconds, or until set around the edges. Add any fillings, then carefully fold the omelet in half.

Vegetable

1 slice ham, chopped

1 tomato, chopped

3 tbsp cooked peas

Handful of fresh spinach leaves

¼ cup roasted red peppers

Ham & tomato

CRUNCHY COATING

SERVE WITH THE DIP OF YOUR CHOICE.

Chicken fingers

🗲 15 mins   ⏱ 25 mins   🍽 Serves 4

This recipe is all about preparation. All you need to do is move the chicken from one bowl to the next to create a delicious, crunchy coating.

Ingredients

¼ cup
all-purpose flour

1 tsp paprika

2 eggs

1 Ask an adult to preheat the oven to 375°F (190°C). Mix the flour and paprika in a bowl and season.

To stop the flour from clumping on your fingers, use one hand to dip into the flour and bread crumbs, and the other to dip into the eggs.

2 Beat the eggs in a second bowl.

3 Combine the bread crumbs and parsley in a third bowl.

4 Dip the chicken strips into each bowl in the order shown here, then place on an oiled baking sheet. Ask an adult to bake the chicken fingers for 20–25 minutes.

  +   +   +

1 cup fine, fresh bread crumbs

2 tbsp freshly chopped flat-leaf parsley

4 boneless, skinless chicken breasts, cut into strips

2 tbsp sunflower oil

Sweet potato fries

Crispy, herby, and very tasty, these sweet potato fries make a great side dish or snack.

CRISPY FRIES

You can peel the potatoes if you like, but you don't have to.

10 mins, plus 1 hr soaking   30 mins   Serves 4

Ingredients

 2 sweet potatoes, about 1lb 2oz (500g), peeled

 2 tbsp olive oil

2 tsp dried mixed herbs

 1 tbsp polenta or cornmeal

 Sea salt

Soaking the potatoes removes starch and helps make them crispy.

1

Cut the potatoes carefully into ¼in (5mm) sticks and soak in cold water for 1 hour. Drain and pat dry with a dish towel.

2

Dried potatoes

Ask an adult to preheat the oven to 425°F (220°C). Mix the herbs and polenta together in a small bowl.

3

Drizzle the oil over the potatoes and add the polenta mixture. Toss to coat and spread out on a nonstick baking sheet.

4

Ask an adult to bake the fries in the oven for about 30 minutes, turning once, until crispy. Sprinkle with sea salt and serve.

Ingredients

 1 cup sushi rice
 +
 1⅓ cups cold water
 +
 2 tbsp rice vinegar
 +
 1 tbsp sugar
 +
 **½ tsp salt**

Sushi rolls

These rice rolls are fun and so easy to make. If you like a bit of spice, then add a little wasabi paste.

SPRINKLE WITH THE SEEDS

For the filling
- ¼ cup mayonnaise
- 2 tsp sriracha sauce
- 1 ripe, but firm, medium avocado, cut in half, pit removed, peeled, and cut into quarters. Cut each quarter into 4 even strips
- Cucumber, seeded, halved lengthwise, and cut into 8 x ½in (1cm) strips

30 mins | 20 mins | Makes 24

1 Gently wash the rice in a strainer with cold water until the water runs clear. Pour the rice and water into a medium saucepan.

2 Ask an adult to bring the rice to a boil, then reduce the heat and cover. Simmer for 10 minutes. Remove from the heat and cover. Let it steam for another 10 minutes.

   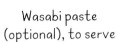

4 sushi seaweed (nori) sheets + 1 bamboo mat + Pickled ginger, to serve + Soy sauce, to serve + 1 tsp black sesame seeds, to serve + Wasabi paste (optional), to serve

In a small bowl, mix together the mayonnaise and sriracha sauce. Set aside. Ask an adult to warm the vinegar, sugar, and salt in a small pan over low heat until dissolved.

Be careful not to crush the rice grains.

Ask an adult to spread the rice over the bottom of a shallow baking pan using a spatula. Pour the vinegar mixture evenly over the rice and gently mix. Let it cool for 20 minutes.

Place a sheet of nori on a bamboo mat, shiny side down. With wet hands, spread a quarter of the rice evenly on the nori. Leave a ½in (1cm) border at the bottom and top.

Spread a thick strip of the mayonnaise horizontally on the rice about 2in (5cm) from the bottom. Place 4 pieces of avocado, widthwise, over the mayo.

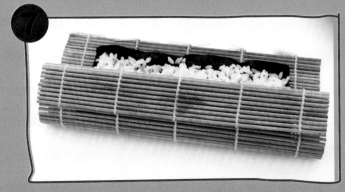

Add 2 strips of cucumber, widthwise, side by side below the avocado. Using the mat, roll the nori tightly from the bottom to the top edge of the nori sheet. Press evenly.

Repeat with the remaining nori to make 3 more rolls. Ask an adult to trim the ends, then slice each roll into 6 pieces, using a sharp, wet paring knife. Serve with the ginger, soy sauce, and wasabi (if using).

23

3 spring onions, finely chopped

Ingredients

+

2 tbsp lime juice

+

6 ripe tomatoes, chopped

+

Small bunch cilantro, chopped

Salsa

Combine the ingredients in a bowl. Season and let sit for no more than 30 minutes before serving. The fresher the salsa, the better it will taste.

Add a drizzle of oil and a sprinkle of paprika (optional).

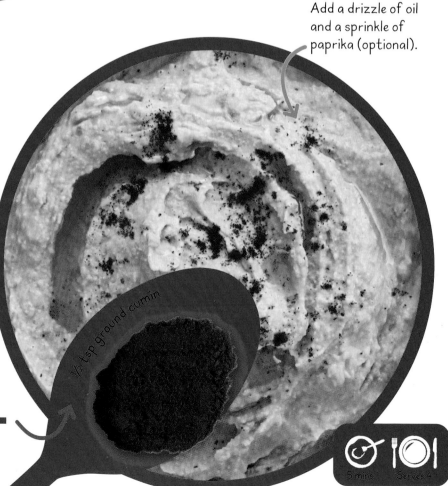

½ tsp ground cumin

Hummus

Place all the ingredients in a food processor and ask an adult to blend them. At 30-second intervals, the mixture needs to be scraped down the sides. Add seasoning and 2–3 tbsp of water and blend until smooth. Transfer to a bowl.

⚠

Ingredients

1 x 14oz (400g) can chickpeas, drained

+

3 tbsp lemon juice

+

½ cup tahini paste

+

1 garlic clove, peeled and crushed

+

Ingredients

½ cucumber, peeled
and seeded

¾ cup
Greek-style yogurt

1 tbsp
lemon juice

1 garlic clove,
crushed

1 tbsp freshly chopped mint

Tzatziki

Grate the cucumber with the help
of an adult, then use paper towels
to squeeze out any excess water.
Mix in a bowl with the rest of the
ingredients. Chill before serving.

2 avocados, pitted and chopped

5 mins   Serves 4

Guacamole

Place the ingredients in a bowl
and crush with a fork or potato
masher. Mash until combined,
leaving some larger avocado
chunks. Season to taste.

Ingredients

¼ cup freshly
chopped cilantro

1 tbsp
lime juice

1 small tomato,
finely chopped

25

Gazpacho

A chilled tomato and cucumber soup from Spain, Gazpacho is very refreshing on a hot summer day.

Garnish with chopped spring onions, small chunks of cucumber, and freshly chopped flat-leaf parsley.

Ingredients

 +  +  +   +

| 3½oz (100g) crusty bread | 2 tbsp red wine vinegar | 2¼lb (1kg) ripe tomatoes, chopped | 1 red and 1 green bell pepper, seeded and coarsely chopped |

1

Vinegar helps bring out the flavor of the tomatoes.

Tear up the bread and place it in a bowl. Pour the vinegar on top and let soak for 10 minutes.

2

Do this in 2 batches. Pour the mixture into a liquid measuring cup.

Ask an adult to blend half the tomatoes, bell peppers, and cucumber with half the garlic and oil in a food processor for 1 minute, then add half the bread and blend until smooth.

3

Repeat with the remaining ingredients and season to taste.

4

Pass the mixture through a strainer into a large bowl, then cover and refrigerate. Serve chilled with fresh garnish. Then cover and refrigerate for 1 hour.

1 cucumber, peeled and coarsely chopped

+

2 garlic cloves

+

¼ cup extra virgin olive oil

Ingredients

2 x 14oz (400g) cans chickpeas, drained + 1 garlic clove, crushed + 2 tsp ground cumin + 1 tsp ground coriander + 2 tbsp freshly chopped flat-leaf parsley

Baked falafel

15 mins, plus 25 mins chilling   20 mins   Serves 4

Crunchy, fluffy, and tasty, falafel is a popular Middle Eastern dish. Falafel are usually fried, but these baked ones are easier to make.

YOGURT DIP

SERVE WITH WARM PITA BREAD. SALAD. AND A YOGURT DIP.

 + + + +

1 tsp baking powder 2 tbsp lemon juice 2 tbsp all-purpose flour 1 tbsp olive oil, plus extra for brushing Pita bread, to serve

1

⚠️ Ask an adult to pulse the chickpeas, garlic, spices, and parsley in a food processor until chopped.

2

⚠️ Season and add the baking powder, lemon juice, flour, and oil. Ask an adult to pulse again until well-combined.

3

⚠️ Divide the mixture into 16 balls and flatten them. Cover and chill in the fridge for 25 minutes. Ask an adult to preheat the oven to 375°F (190°C).

4

⚠️ Brush a baking sheet with the oil. Ask an adult to bake the falafel on the sheet for 10 minutes, then turn them over and bake for another 5–10 minutes.

For the dip
- ½ cup Greek yogurt
- 2 tbsp chopped mint
- ¼ cucumber, finely chopped

29

Ingredients

 +
 +
 +
 +

14oz (400g) butternut squash, peeled and cubed

1 zucchini, cut into 1in (2.5cm) chunks

1 red onion, cut into 8 wedges

1 red bell pepper, seeded and cut into 1in (2.5cm) pieces

Roasted veggie & couscous salad

⌀ 15 mins | 🕐 40 mins | 🍽 Serves 4

Serve this healthy dish warm as a main dish, or cold as a side dish with grilled chicken or fish.

2

Ask an adult to roast the vegetables for 15 minutes, then carefully turn everything over so the food cooks evenly. Return to the oven and cook for another 15–20 minutes.

Try to get all the vegetables in 1 layer.

1

Ask an adult to prepare the squash (see page 138) and preheat the oven to 400°F (200°C). Scatter the squash, zucchini, onion, and bell pepper into a roasting pan. Drizzle with the olive oil and season.

3

Place the couscous in a large bowl with the lemon zest and juice. Ask an adult to add the stock, stir, cover, and let stand for 5 minutes. Season to taste and gently fluff with a fork.

1 tbsp olive oil + 1 cup couscous + 1¼ cups hot vegetable stock + Zest and juice of 2 lemons + ¼ cup freshly chopped mixed herbs

4

Mix the vegetables and herbs into the couscous.

GREAT TO EAT HOT OR COLD!

Crispy chickpeas

These baked chickpeas are a simple snack. The base recipe uses just salt and pepper, but you can add more flavorings to switch things up.

1

Ask an adult to preheat the oven to 400°F (200°C). Place the chickpeas on a rimmed baking sheet and dry them with paper towels. Remove any loose skins.

5 mins   30 mins   Serves 4–6

Variations

Cook the chickpeas as shown above, adding the flavorings before returning them to the oven to crisp for the last 30 minutes.

2 tsp dried mixed herbs

3 tbsp Parmesan cheese, grated

Moroccan

Herb & Parmesan

2

Mix the oil, sea salt, and freshly ground black pepper in a bowl and pour onto the chickpeas. Stir to coat.

Ingredients

2 x 14oz (400g) cans chickpeas, drained and rinsed

+

1 tbsp olive oil

+

2 tsp sea salt

+

1 tsp freshly ground black pepper

3

Ask an adult to roast the chickpeas for 30 minutes, stirring once to ensure even cooking. Turn off the oven and leave in there for 30 minutes to crisp up.

2 tbsp Moroccan spice mixture

Salt & pepper

Honey & cinnamon

For this variation, don't include the salt and pepper.

1 tsp ground cinnamon and 2 tbsp honey

Ingredients

3½oz (100g) dried rice
vermicelli noodles

+

12 x 7in (18cm)
dried rice paper rounds

+

24 mint leaves and
24 cilantro leaves

+

18 cooked and peeled
medium shrimp,
halved lengthwise

+

1 carrot, peeled and
cut into thin strips

+

1 small red bell pepper,
halved, seeded, and
cut into thin strips

+

4 green onions, thinly
sliced lengthwise

Summer rolls

These rice paper rolls make a perfect
light, fresh-tasting snack. Try them with
cooked, shredded chicken or extra
veggies, if you like.

Make in advance so
the flavors mingle.
Put in the fridge
under a damp cloth
until ready to serve.

**For the
dipping sauce**
- 5 tbsp sweet
  chili sauce
- 2 tbsp lime juice

20 mins   Makes 12

1

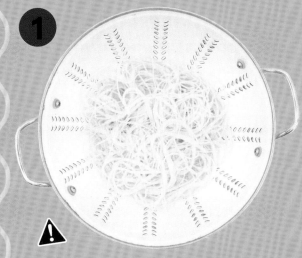

⚠️

Ask an adult to place the noodles in a bowl and pour in boiling water to cover. Let stand for 5 minutes, or until the noodles have softened. Drain well.

2

Place each wrapper (rice paper round), one at a time, in a bowl of warm water to soften and turn clear. Remove and shake off excess water.

3

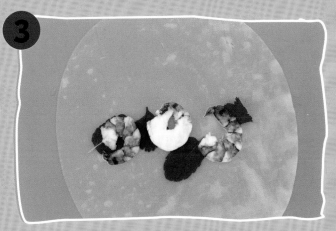

Place a wrapper on a clean work surface, add 2 mint leaves and 2 cilantro leaves, then place 3 shrimp halves in the center.

4

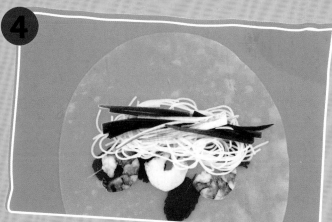

Add some of the noodles, just above the shrimp, and top with the carrot, red bell pepper, and green onion strips.

5

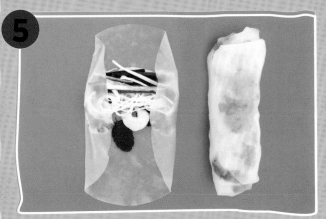

Fold in the side edges to the filling. Bring the bottom edge over and roll to make a package. Cover with a damp cloth.

6

Repeat Steps 3 to 5 to make the remaining rolls. For the dipping sauce, combine the sweet chili sauce and lime juice in a small bowl.

35

Lunch wraps

A great alternative to sandwiches, wraps can be filled with your favorite ingredients. These are easy to make (see pages 38–39), but first you'll need to do a little prep work.

⚠️ Ask an adult to assist you in cutting the vegetables.

WRAPS MAKE GREAT, HEALTHY PACKED LUNCHES.

Bell pepper

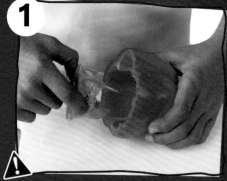

Keep your fingers tucked away safely.

1 Slice off the top carefully and pull out the seeds.

2 Cut into four sections. Take care with the sharp knife.

3 Carefully trim any pith and slice into thin strips.

Carrot

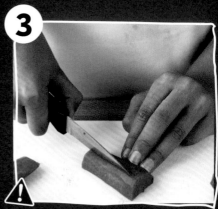

1 Peel a carrot and cut off the top and bottom.

2 Carefully chop the carrot into medium-sized chunks.

3 Slice the chunks lengthwise into sticks carefully.

Beets

Beets can be a little messy, so watch out!

1 Cut a cooked beet in half carefully.

2 Using caution, cut each half into slices.

3 Carefully slice them into smaller pieces.

Ingredients

1 large
flour tortilla
+
Cream cheese
+
Handful of baby
spinach leaves
+
1 beet, cooked
and sliced
+
½ yellow bell pepper,
seeded and sliced
+
½ carrot,
peeled and sliced

Rolling your wraps

Take your
prepped vegetables
and roll them up, as shown.
Then try out the recipes
on the next page,
or create your own
wrap recipe.

1 Spread a layer of cream
cheese onto a tortilla.

2 Arrange your rainbow of
chopped vegetables on top.

READY
TO EAT!

3 Fold in three edges
of the tortilla.

4 Roll from the closed
end to close the wrap.

5 Ask an adult to neatly
slice the wrap in half.

Ingredients

1 large
flour tortilla

+

Mayonnaise

+

2 strips bacon,
cooked

+

Handful of
lettuce leaves

+

3 cherry
tomatoes, halved

BLT

This crispy wrap is a great alternative to the classic BLT sandwich. Do you know what "BLT" stands for? It means bacon, lettuce, and tomato!

5 mins   Makes 1

Hummus avocado

This yummy wrap is full of healthy greens that go perfectly with the creamy hummus.

5 mins   Makes 1

Ingredients

1 large
flour tortilla

+

Hummus

+

1 avocado, peeled
and cut into strips

+

¼ cucumber,
sliced

+

Handful of
arugula leaves

39

Ingredients

4 large beefsteak tomatoes,
about 9oz (250g) each

+

1 tsp salt

+

2 tbsp olive oil

+

1 small
onion, chopped

Stuffed tomatoes

15 mins   45 mins   Makes 4

Vegetables stuffed with meat are popular in
lots of countries. This version comes from France,
where it is called *Tomates farcies*.

TOMATO HATS!

Cook the
tomatoes
in a baking
dish to catch
the juices.

+ **1 garlic clove, crushed**

+ **1lb (450g) good quality sausages**

+ **4 tbsp freshly chopped flat-leaf parsley**

+ **1 tbsp freshly chopped thyme**

1

The salt draws out excess liquid.

Ask an adult to cut a ¾in (2cm) thick slice off the top of each tomato and scoop out the insides. Save the tops for later.

2

Sprinkle a little salt into the tomatoes and turn them upside down. Ask an adult to heat 1 tbsp of the oil in a small pan and cook the onion and garlic over low heat for 2–3 minutes until soft.

3

Ask an adult to preheat the oven to 400°F (200°C). Squeeze the meat out of the sausage casings into a bowl. Mix in the onion, garlic, and herbs, then season.

4

Rinse out the salt, then stuff the mixture into the tomatoes. Put the tops back on and drizzle with the remaining oil. Ask an adult to cook the tomatoes for 45 minutes.

Ingredients

2 small avocados, destoned and diced + 2 tbsp fresh cilantro, chopped + 2 tbsp lime juice + 2 tbsp olive oil +

Quesadillas

Gooey quesadillas are quick to make and totally tasty. These are filled with black beans and avocado, but there are two delicious variations to try on pages 44–45.

5 mins · **10 mins** · **Serves 2**

1

Lime juice stops the avocado from turning brown.

Mash the avocado in a bowl, then add the cilantro and lime juice. Season with salt and freshly ground black pepper. Set aside.

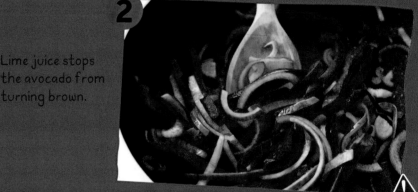

2

⚠️

Ask an adult to heat half the oil in a pan over medium heat and cook the onion and bell pepper for 2–3 minutes, until softened.

3

⚠️

Ask an adult to add the beans and season with salt and freshly ground black pepper. Cook for about 2 minutes and set aside.

4

Spread half the avocado mixture onto half of one of the tortillas, then top with the bell pepper and bean mixture.

½ red onion, sliced

+

 ½ red bell pepper, seeded and sliced

+

 ½ x 14oz (400g) can black beans, drained

+

2 large flour tortillas

+

 1¾oz (50g) Cheddar cheese, grated

SERVE WITH SALSA.

5 Repeat with the other tortilla and sprinkle cheese on top. Fold both tortillas in half to make half-moon shapes.

6 Ask an adult to heat the remaining oil over low heat and fry the quesadillas for 2 minutes on each side, or until golden brown.

The half-moon shape keeps the filling from falling out when flipping.

 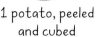 

| 2 large flour tortillas | + | 1 tbsp olive oil | + | 1 potato, peeled and cubed | + | 1 onion, chopped | + | 3½oz (100g) chorizo, diced | + | 2½oz (75g) Cheddar cheese, grated |

More quesadillas

5 mins | 15 mins | Serves 2

Once you know how to make quesadillas, you can get creative with the fillings. After you try these two, why not come up with your own versions?

⚠ Chorizo & potato

Ask an adult to heat the oil in a pan and cook the potato for 10 minutes, until softened. Add the onion and chorizo and cook for another 2–3 minutes. Fill and cook as shown on the previous page.

Chicken & corn ⚠

Spread the salsa onto one half of each tortilla and top with the rest of the ingredients. Ask an adult to fry the quesadillas as shown in Step 6 on page 43.

5 mins | 5 mins | Serves 2

Ingredients

2 large flour tortillas + ¼ cup salsa + ½ cup cooked, shredded chicken + ¾ cup corn + ½ red bell pepper, seeded and chopped + 2½oz (75g) Cheddar cheese, grated

1 lb 2 oz (500g) store-bought pie dough

+

3 eggs

+

¾ cup heavy cream

+

¾ cup milk

+

Cheesy quiche

This classic tart originated in France, where it is called *Quiche Lorraine*. It's light and yummy, and a great way to practice using dough.

For this recipe, you will need a loose-bottomed 9in (23cm) quiche pan and baking beans.

CUT INTO SLICES AND SERVE WITH A SALAD.

Pinch of nutmeg

+

7oz (200g) cooked
bacon, chopped

+

3½oz (100g)
Gruyère, grated

1

Ask an adult to preheat the oven to 375°F (190°C). Roll out the dough and line a loose-bottomed 9in (23cm) quiche pan. Chill for 15 minutes and carefully prick the dough with a fork.

2

> This is called "blind baking." It stops the dough from getting soggy when the filling is added.

Line with parchment paper and fill with the baking beans. Place on a baking sheet and ask an adult to bake the dough for 15 minutes. Carefully remove the paper and beans and bake for another 5 minutes.

3

Whisk together the eggs, cream, milk, and nutmeg. Transfer to a liquid measuring cup.

5

Pour the egg mixture on top and sprinkle with the remaining cheese. Ask an adult to bake the quiche for 25–30 minutes. Remove from the oven and let cool for 5 minutes.

4

Ask an adult to remove the pie dish from the oven and scatter the bacon and half the cheese over the quiche crust.

Ingredients

1 tbsp sunflower oil	1 onion, diced	1 red and 1 green bell pepper, seeded and diced	1 garlic clove, crushed	1 tsp chili powder 1 tsp dried oregano

Beef tacos

These tasty tacos are a quick and filling meal for any night of the week. For fresh fillings, make your own salsa on page 24 and guacamole on page 25.

10 mins   36 mins   Serves 4

FILL THEM UP!

For the filling
- Crispy lettuce, such as iceberg, thinly shredded
- Salsa
- Guacamole
- Cheddar cheese, grated
- Lime wedges

48

  +  + + +

1 tsp ground paprika,
2 tsp ground cumin

1lb 2oz (500g)
ground beef

1 cup
hot beef stock

2 tbsp freshly
chopped cilantro

12 flour
taco tortillas

1

Cook the onion and bell peppers
until softened, but not browned.

Ask an adult to heat the oil in a
large frying pan over medium heat.
Add the onion and bell peppers.
Cook gently for 8 minutes.

2

Ask an adult to stir in the garlic and spices and
cook gently for 2–3 minutes. Add the ground
beef. Cook over medium heat for 5 minutes
until browned.

3

Ask an adult to pour in the stock.
Season with salt and freshly ground
black pepper. Simmer uncovered for
20 minutes, stirring occasionally, until
reduced. Mix in the cilantro.

4

Serve the
tacos with a
squeeze of lime
juice for a
tangy flavor.

Ask an adult to warm the tortillas
according to package instructions.
Load up the tortillas with the spiced
beef, shredded lettuce, salsa,
guacamole, and grated cheese.

49

Ingredients

 Olive oil, for greasing

+

 1¼ cups all-purpose flour

+

 1 tsp baking powder

+

 1 tsp dried oregano

+

 8 tbsp butter, melted

Pizza muffins

These easy, cheesy treats are a tasty twist on pizza. They're great on their own, but even better with a yummy dipping sauce.

For this recipe, you will need a 12-hole muffin pan.

15 mins · 25 mins · Makes 8–10

SPRINKLE WITH BASIL.

DIP IN PIZZA SAUCE.

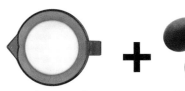
1 cup milk

2 eggs

2 tbsp pizza sauce, plus extra for dipping

4oz (115g) mixed Cheddar and mozzarella cheese, grated

5½oz (150g) mini pepperoni, sliced

1

The oil stops the muffins from sticking.

Ask an adult to preheat the oven to 375°F (190°C). Grease the muffin pan with the oil.

2

Mix thoroughly.

Mix the flour, baking powder, and oregano in a bowl, and the butter, milk, eggs, and pizza sauce in a liquid measuring cup.

3

Pour the egg mixture into the flour mixture and lightly stir together. Then fold in the cheese and pepperoni.

4

Only fill the cups up ¾ of the way full or the mix will spill out.

Spoon the mixture into the muffin pan. Ask an adult to bake the pizza muffins for 20–25 minutes, until golden.

51

Main dishes

There's nothing quite like a delicious, satisfying meal. So, learn to cook your favorite dishes, and dinner will always feel special.

1¼ cups dried macaroni

+

5½oz (150g) cream cheese

+

1¾ cups milk

+

1 tsp Dijon mustard

+

6oz (175g) Cheddar cheese, grated

+

8 cherry tomatoes, halved

Mac & cheese

Almost everyone loves mac and cheese! And this clever "cheat's" way to make it couldn't be simpler.

5 mins   30 mins   Serves 4

SERVE WITH A CRISP GREEN SALAD.

1 Ask an adult to preheat the oven to 375°F (190°C). Cook the pasta in a pan of lightly salted boiling water for 7-9 minutes. Carefully drain and transfer to an ovenproof dish.

2 Mix the cream cheese, milk, mustard, and half the Cheddar cheese in a bowl. Season. Whisk until smooth.

3 Pour the sauce over the pasta and mix. Sprinkle the remaining cheese and tomatoes on top. Ask an adult to bake the dish in the oven for 20 minutes, or until golden and bubbly.

Fried rice

Making fried rice is a simple and fantastic way to turn leftover rice into something exciting

1 Ask an adult to heat the oil in a wok. Add the rice, peas, and bell pepper, and carefully cook for 3-4 minutes.

2 Ask an adult to push the rice mixture to one side and pour the egg into the wok.

3 Let the egg set for 10 seconds. An adult should then break up the set egg into the rice.

5 mins   8 mins   Serves 4

Ingredients

 2 tbsp sunflower oil

+

2 cups cooked long-grain rice

+

 ½ cup frozen peas

+

 ½ red bell pepper, seeded and finely sliced

+

56

4

Ask an adult to stir in the corn, spring onions, bean sprouts, and soy sauce, and cook for another 2–3 minutes.

PACKED WITH FLAVOR!

  2 eggs, beaten

+

 ½ cup corn

+

4 spring onions, chopped

+

 1 cup bean sprouts

+

  2 tbsp light soy sauce

1

This removes excess water from the tofu.

Place the tofu between two sheets of paper towels and put something heavy on top for 15 minutes.

2

Ask an adult to cut the tofu into 1in (2.5cm) cubes and combine with the oil, garlic, lemon juice, vinegar, and herbs. Marinate for 1 hour.

3

Ask an adult to preheat the broiler to medium. Carefully thread the tofu and vegetables onto skewers.

4

Ask an adult to broil the kebabs for 5–6 minutes, then carefully turn and brush with any remaining marinade. Cook for another 5 minutes.

Ingredients

 14oz (400g) firm tofu

+

 2 tbsp olive oil

+

 1 garlic clove, crushed

+

 2 tbsp lemon juice

+

Tofu kebabs

These kebabs are simple and healthy.
Try varying the vegetables by
adding mushrooms or
cubes of zucchini.

20 mins, plus
1 hr marinating

11 mins

Makes 4

1 tbsp red
wine vinegar

2 tsp dried
mixed herbs

1 small red onion,
cut into 8 wedges

1 small yellow bell
pepper, seeded and
cut into cubes

8 cherry
tomatoes

59

Ingredients

1 cup
bread flour

+

½ tsp salt

+

½ tsp
dried yeast

+

½ cup
warm water

+

1 tbsp extra virgin olive
oil, plus extra for greasing

+

2 tbsp pizza sauce

+

2 tbsp grated
Cheddar cheese

+

4½oz (125g) mozzarella,
drained and sliced

+

2 tomatoes, sliced

60

Perfect pizza

It's easy to make pizza from scratch. Here's a basic
recipe to make one pizza crust. The variations for
toppings are endless. See pages 62–63 for inspiration.

1

Combine the flour, salt, and
yeast in a bowl. Make a well
and add the water and oil.

2

Mix until the dough
comes together, then knead
for 10 minutes until smooth.

3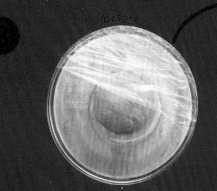

Before / After

Brush a clean bowl with oil.
Place the dough in the bowl
and cover with plastic wrap.

Let rise for an hour, or until
the dough has doubled in size.
Ask an adult to preheat the oven
to 425°F (220°C).

4

Place on a lightly greased
baking sheet, then roll the
dough into a 10in (25cm) circle.

5

Spread on the sauce and
top with the cheese and tomatoes.
Ask an adult to bake the pizza
for 10–15 minutes.

15 mins, plus 1 hr proofing

15 mins

Makes 1

SPRINKLE
WITH BASIL.

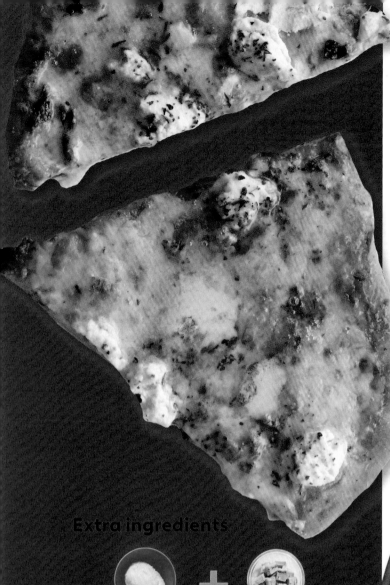

Ham & mushroom

Spread pizza sauce on the base and scatter the rest of the ingredients on top. Add oregano, if you like.

Extra ingredients

1¾oz (50g)
ham, sliced

1¾oz (50g)
mushrooms, sliced

1¾oz (50g)
Cheddar cheese,
grated

Extra ingredients

1¾oz (50g)
mozzarella, sliced

1¾oz (50g)
Gorgonzola
cheese, cubed

2oz (60g)
ricotta cheese

1oz (25g)
Parmesan
cheese, grated

Four cheese

Omit the pizza sauce. Layer the mozzarella and Gorgonzola around the base. Top with teaspoons of ricotta, then scatter with the Parmesan.

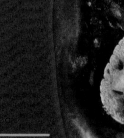

Pepper & pepperoni

Spread pizza sauce on the base and sprinkle the cheese on top. Add the pepperoni and bell pepper slices.

Extra ingredients

3½oz (100g)
mozzarella, grated

3½oz (100g)
pepperoni, sliced

½ green bell pepper,
½ red bell pepper,
seeded and sliced

Extra ingredients

½oz (15g)
Parmesan
cheese, grated

3½oz (100g)
baby spinach, wilted

3½oz (100g)
ricotta cheese

Spinach & ricotta

Spread the base with pizza sauce and sprinkle with Parmesan. Top with the spinach and spoonfuls of ricotta.

Ingredients

 2 tbsp
butter, softened

+

 1 tsp grated
lemon zest

+

 1 tbsp freshly
chopped dill

+

 1¾oz (50g) green
beans, trimmed

 10 mins 25 mins Serves 2

Salmon parcels

Fish is healthy and delicious, but can be tricky to cook. However, it's super simple if you cook it in parchment paper.

The fish steams in the moisture trapped by the parchment paper parcel.

SQUEEZE THE LEMON OVER THE FISH.

+

1¾oz (50g) snow peas or
sugar snap peas, trimmed

+

1¾oz (50g)
baby spinach

+

2 boneless, skinless
salmon fillets

+

2 lemon
wedges

1

Ask an adult to preheat the oven to
400°F (200°C). Cut 2 large squares
of parchment paper. Mix the butter,
lemon zest, and dill in a small bowl.

2

Stack half the vegetables in the center
of one of the sheets of parchment paper,
leaving space around the edges.

3

Place a piece of salmon on
the vegetables and add half the
butter mixture on top.

4

Add a lemon wedge, repeat, and seal both
parcels by folding them up and twisting the
ends. Ask an adult to bake for 20–25 minutes.

Ingredients

| 2 tsp vegetable oil | 3 tbsp Thai green curry paste | 1 x 13.5fl oz (400ml) can of coconut milk | 1 tsp light soy sauce | 2 fresh makrut lime leaves, coarsely torn |

Thai green curry

Use a ready-made Thai curry paste to make this spicy coconut curry packed with vegetables.

5 mins   25 mins   Serves 4

To serve
- Basmati or Jasmine rice
- Lime wedges

STEAM THE RICE ACCORDING TO THE INSTRUCTIONS ON THE PACKAGE.

½lb (225g) baby new potatoes, cut into ¾in (2cm) pieces

+

5½oz (150g) snow peas

+

1 red bell pepper, halved, seeded, and cut into strips

+

1 x 8oz (225g) can of bamboo shoots, drained

+

Handful of Thai basil or cilantro leaves

1 Ask an adult to heat the oil in a large saucepan. Add the curry paste. Cook for 1–2 minutes, stirring constantly. Add the coconut milk, soy sauce, and lime leaves.

Occasionally stir the potatoes.

2 Ask an adult to bring it to a boil, then cover and simmer for 2 minutes. Stir in the potatoes, cover, and simmer for 15 minutes until they are just tender.

3 Stir in the snow peas, bell pepper strips, and bamboo shoots. Cover and simmer for 2–3 minutes, stirring once, until all the vegetables are tender.

4 Stir in the Thai basil leaves or cilantro. Serve immediately in bowls alongside steamed rice and lime wedges.

Ingredients

 +  + +

1 onion, sliced	1¼lb (500g) mini new potatoes	14oz (400g) carrots, peeled and cut into chunks	7oz (200g) button mushrooms	8 pork sausages

Sausage bake

This hearty dish is so easy to make. All you need to do is add all the ingredients to a dish and let the oven do the rest!

Slice any larger potatoes in half, so the food cooks evenly.

1 Ask an adult to preheat the oven to 350°F (180°C). Place the onion, potatoes, carrots, and mushrooms into an ovenproof dish.

ONE-DISH WONDER!

2 Place the sausages on top and drizzle with the oil. Ask an adult to mix the stock with the tomato paste and the dash of sauce and pour it all in the dish.

3 Ask an adult to season the dish and bake it in the oven for 30 minutes, then stir and bake for another 30 minutes.

+ 1 tbsp olive oil

+ 1¾ cups (400ml) hot beef stock

+ 1 tsp tomato paste

+ Dash of soy or Worcestershire sauce

SERVE WITH PEAS, GREEN BEANS, OR BROCCOLI.

For extra color and flavor, sprinkle with freshly chopped flat-leaf parsley before serving.

Spiced rice

15 mins · 20 mins · Serves 4

Cooking rice in a delicious sauce is a great way to give it lots of extra flavor.

TOP WITH A FRIED EGG.

Ingredients

1 cup long grain rice

+

2 tbsp vegetable oil

+

1 onion, finely chopped

+

2 garlic cloves, crushed

+

1 green bell pepper, seeded and finely chopped

1

Ask an adult to cook the rice according to the package instructions, then drain.

2

Ask an adult to heat the oil in a large frying pan over medium heat and cook the onion and garlic for 3–4 minutes. Add the bell pepper and cook for 2–3 minutes.

3

Stir in the cumin, oregano, bay leaf, and tomatoes and cook for 4–5 minutes.

4

Take the bay leaf out before serving.

Add the tomato puree. Ask an adult to cook for 4–5 minutes on low heat and then stir the rice into the sauce.

+ ½ tsp ground cumin + 1 tsp dried oregano + 1 bay leaf + 2 tomatoes, chopped + ¾ cup tomato puree

71

Caesar salad

This classic dish combines delicious chicken, crispy lettuce, crunchy croutons, and a rich, creamy sauce.

TOP WITH SHAVINGS OF PARMESAN CHEESE.

Ask an adult to preheat the oven to 375°F (190°C). Coat the bread with oil and a little sea salt.

Ask an adult to bake the bread for about 10 minutes, until it's golden and crunchy.

Ask an adult to cook the chicken in a grill pan for 7 minutes on each side, or until fully cooked through. An adult should then cut it into strips.

Mix in 1 tbsp of the dressing at a time so you don't add too much.

Place the lettuce in a bowl and mix in the dressing, chicken, and bread.

Ingredients

 +   + + +

2 slices crusty bread, torn or cut into pieces   2 tbsp olive oil, plus extra for coating   Sea salt   2 small boneless skinless chicken breasts   1 Romaine lettuce, chopped   Caesar dressing, to serve

Ingredients

 1 tbsp olive oil + 1 red onion, thinly sliced +  1 garlic clove, crushed +  2 celery ribs, trimmed and sliced + 2 carrots, peeled and sliced + 2 x 14oz (400g) cans cannelli beans, drained and rinsed +

White bean stew

Packed with yummy veggies, this stew is perfect for a cold, rainy day. For an added crunch, don't forget the garlic toasts!

 10 mins   32 mins   Serves 4

1 Stir occasionally until it starts to soften, but not color.

Ask an adult to heat the oil in a large pan. Add the onion, garlic, celery, and carrots and cook over medium-low heat for 4–5 minutes.

2 Stir occasionally as it simmers.

Add the beans, pesto, tomatoes, stock, rosemary, and seasoning. Ask an adult to bring it to a boil, reduce the heat, and cover and simmer for 15 minutes.

3

For the garlic toasts, mix the butter, garlic, and parsley until well-combined. Season with salt and freshly ground black pepper. Ask an adult to preheat the broiler to high.

4

Ask an adult to broil the bread on one side. Turn over and spread with the garlic butter. Return to the broiler and cook for 2–3 minutes, or until golden.

| 2 tbsp sundried tomato pesto | 1 x 14oz (400g) can chopped tomatoes | 2 cups hot vegetable stock | 1 tbsp freshly chopped rosemary | ¼lb (150g) cavolo nero kale, trimmed and coarsely chopped | Grated zest of 1 lemon |

5

⚠️

Add the kale to the stew and cover. Ask an adult to cook it for another 5–6 minutes until the vegetables are tender. Stir in the lemon zest and season to taste.

For the garlic toasts
- 4 tbsp butter, softened
- 1 garlic clove, peeled and crushed
- 2 tbsp freshly chopped parsley
- 8 x 1in (2.5cm) slices French bread

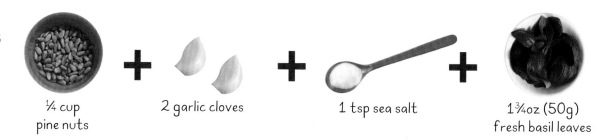

¼ cup
pine nuts

+

2 garlic cloves

+

1 tsp sea salt

+

1¾oz (50g)
fresh basil leaves

Pasta with pesto

Fresh pesto is so much better than store-bought.
A fresh batch like this should keep in the fridge
for up to a week.

10 mins   12 mins   Serves 4

CREAMY
SAUCE

FRESH
BASIL

 **+** **+** **+**  **+**

4½oz (125g) Parmesan
cheese, freshly grated

¾ cup extra
virgin olive oil

12oz (350g)
dried spaghetti

Freshly ground
black pepper

1

Ask an adult to toast the
pine nuts in a dry pan over
medium heat for 2–3 minutes.

2

Ask an adult to pulse
the pine nuts, garlic,
sea salt, and basil in
a food processor until
you have a silky paste.

3

Transfer to a bowl and
mix in the cheese.

4

Using a spoon, beat in the
olive oil a little at a time until
you have a thick sauce.

5

Ask an adult to boil the pasta in
a pan of lightly salted water for
8–10 minutes. Drain, reserving a
little bit of the pasta water.

6

RESERVED
WATER

Return the pasta to the pan and mix
in half of the pesto. Add the reserved
water to help bind everything together,
then add pepper.

1

Place all the ingredients except the oil in a bowl and mix until combined.

🎯 15 mins   ⏱ 24 mins   🍽 Makes 24

2

Roll into 24 balls. Ask an adult to brown them in oil in a large frying pan over a medium heat for 10–12 minutes. ⚠

Meatballs are a really versatile ingredient. There are recipes on pages 80–84 that you can use either of these versions with.

Meatballs

Cook the meatballs in two batches so they brown better.

Ingredients

7oz (200g) lean ground beef

+

7oz (200g) ground pork

+

2 tbsp Parmesan cheese, grated

+

2 tbsp freshly chopped flat-leaf parsley

+

1 tsp dried oregano

+

1 tbsp dried bread crumbs

+

1 egg, beaten

+

2 tbsp olive oil

Ingredients

2 tbsp olive oil

+

1 onion, chopped

+

1 garlic clove, crushed

+

9oz (250g) mushrooms, finely chopped

+

1 x 14oz (400g) can green lentils, drained and rinsed

+

6 tbsp dried bread crumbs

+

2 tbsp freshly chopped flat-leaf parsley

+

2 tsp dried mixed herbs

+

1 egg, beaten

Veggie balls

1

Ask an adult to heat 1 tbsp of the oil in a pan and cook the onion, garlic, and mushrooms for 5 minutes.

2

Ask an adult to put the mixture in a food processor, add the remaining ingredients, and pulse until combined. Transfer to a bowl and chill for 30 minutes.

3

Roll into 24 balls. Ask an adult to cook the balls in 2 batches. Add the remaining oil to a large frying pan and cook the balls over a medium heat for 10–12 minutes, turning often.

15 mins, plus 30 mins chilling   17 mins   Makes 24

Meatball ciabatta

This delicious, hot sandwich is a fun and creative way to use your meat or veggie balls from pages 78–79.

1

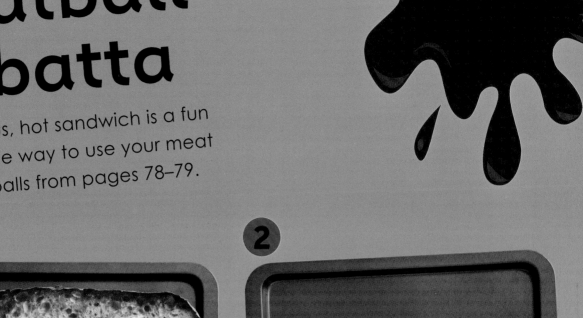

Ask an adult to lightly toast both sides of the bread under the broiler.

2

Carefully spread a layer of pizza sauce over one half of the bread.

3

Arrange the cooked meat or veggie balls on top and ask an adult to broil for 2 minutes.

4

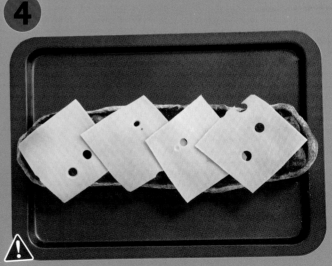

Lay the cheese on top. Ask an adult to return to the broiler for 2–3 minutes. Place the other half of the bread on top and carefully cut into four portions.

Ingredients

1 ciabatta, halved
lengthwise

+

6 tbsp pizza
or pasta sauce

+

Meat or veggie balls
from pages 78–79

+

4 slices Emmental or
other melting cheese

5 mins   10 mins   Serves 4

SERVE WITH
ARUGULA.

Spaghetti & meatballs

Put either your meat or veggie balls from pages 78–79 to good use with this hearty and delicious pasta dish.

5 mins 30 mins Serves 4

Ask an adult to heat the oil in a large pan and gently cook the onion and garlic for 4–5 minutes.

Stir in the tomatoes, puree, oregano, and sugar, then add ¾ cup of water. Season with salt and freshly ground black pepper.

Ask an adult to bring to a boil, then simmer uncovered for 15 minutes. Ask them to add the cooked meat or veggie balls and cook for another 7–8 minutes.

Ingredients

 + + + +

1 tbsp olive oil   1 onion, sliced   1 garlic clove, crushed   1 x 14oz (400g) can chopped tomatoes

4

The pasta should be tender but still firm to the bite and not soggy.

⚠️

Ask an adult to boil the pasta in a pan of lightly salted water for 8–10 minutes and then drain. Use tongs to transfer the pasta to the pan and combine.

Sprinkle with grated Parmesan cheese and basil leaves.

1¼ cups tomato puree + 1 tsp dried oregano + 1 tsp sugar + Meat or veggie balls from pages 78–79 + 12oz (350g) dried spaghetti

Minty kebabs

The secret to this recipe is the flavorful marinade. If you make this dish a day ahead of time, it'll taste even better.

10 mins, plus 1 hr marinating | 15 mins | Makes 5

SPRINKLE WITH FRESH MINT.

SPRINKLE FETA ON TOP.

Serve with salad greens and lemon wedges.

Ingredients

¾ cup plain yogurt

+

1 tbsp olive oil

+

2 tbsp lemon juice

1

Mix the yogurt, oil, lemon juice, mint, and paprika in a bowl. Season with salt and freshly ground black pepper.

2

Full of flavor!

Add the lamb and stir to coat. Leave in the fridge to marinate for an hour, or overnight.

Soaking wooden skewers keeps them from burning.

3

⚠

Carefully thread the lamb onto wooden skewers that have been soaked in water. Ask an adult to set the broiler to high and cook the kebabs for 6–7 minutes.

4

Check page 25 for a tzatziki dip that's perfect with these kebabs.

⚠

Ask an adult to turn the kebabs and brush with the remaining marinade. Then broil for another 6–7 minutes, or until the meat is cooked through.

 +  +  +

¼ cup freshly chopped mint

1 tsp paprika

12oz (350g) lamb, cut into cubes

1¾oz (50g) feta cheese, crumbled

Ingredients

 1 tbsp dark
soy sauce

+

 3 tbsp
honey

+

 2 tsp whole-grain
mustard

+

 2 tsp olive oil

+

10 mins | 40 mins | Serves 4

Sticky chicken

This simple meal is all cooked
in one pan, so it's great for a
dinner when you're after flavor
without lots of dirty dishes!

STICKY
SAUCE

Goes well with
a green salad,
but it's delicious
on its own, too!

 **8 boneless, skinless chicken thighs** +  **3 carrots, peeled and quartered** +  **3 parsnips, peeled and quartered** +  **A few sprigs of thyme**

1

⚠️ Ask an adult to preheat the oven to 400°F (200°C). Mix the soy sauce, honey, mustard, and oil in a bowl. Add the chicken and stir.

2

Place the carrots and parsnips in a baking pan and lay the chicken on top. Season with salt and freshly ground black pepper, add the thyme, and pour the sauce over the dish.

3

Sticky and delicious!

⚠️ Ask an adult to roast the chicken dish for 20 minutes, then remove from the oven and stir. Ask them to return the pan to the oven and cook for another 20 minutes, or until the chicken is cooked through.

BEFORE SERVING, SPOON ANY REMAINING SAUCE ON TOP OF THE CHICKEN.

Ingredients

6 sweet Italian sausages

+

1 tbsp olive oil

+

2 tbsp unsalted butter

+

1 onion, finely chopped

+

1 garlic clove, crushed

+

¾lb (300g) peeled butternut squash, cut into ½in (1.5 cm) cubes

Sausage risotto

Risotto is a delicious meal for the whole family. The trick to success is to keep stirring while all the liquid absorbs. Get those arm muscles working!

1

Squeeze the sausages out of their casings. Ask an adult to cut them into chunks. Heat the oil and butter in a large pan.

2

Ask an adult to stir in the onion. Add the garlic and sweat gently for 2–3 minutes, until softened but not colored, stirring occasionally.

Use a wooden spoon to break up the sausages.

3

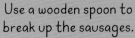

See page 138 to learn how to prepare squash.

Add the sausage chunks and cook for 4–5 minutes, until browned. Stir in the butternut squash and rosemary. Cook for another 4–5 minutes, until it starts to brown.

4

Stir in the rice and cook for 2 minutes, until the rice is shiny and the edges of the grains start to look transparent.

 2 tsp chopped rosemary

 1½ cups arborio or risotto rice

 4½ cups hot chicken stock

 4 tbsp chopped flat-leaf parsley

 ¼ cup grated Parmesan cheese, plus extra to serve

SPRINKLE WITH PARMESAN CHEESE

Cover and let stand for a few minutes before serving.

5 Ask an adult to stir in the hot stock, ½ cup at a time, stirring constantly, until most of the liquid has been absorbed. This should take about 18–20 minutes.

6 The risotto is ready when the butternut squash and rice grains are tender. Season well with salt and freshly ground black pepper. Stir in the parsley and Parmesan.

Ingredients

 + + + ... + ...

1 tbsp olive oil	1 onion, chopped	1 garlic clove, crushed	1 large potato, peeled and cut into small chunks	2 carrots, peeled and cut into small chunks

Chunky vegetable soup

Warming, comforting, and packed with healthy vegetables, this soup is the perfect dish for a cold evening.

SERVE WITH CRUSTY BREAD.

LOTS OF CHUNKY VEGETABLES!

10 mins   30 mins   Serves 4

  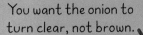 

| 1 tsp ground paprika | 1 x 14oz (400g) can chopped tomatoes | 4¼ cups hot vegetable stock | 7oz (200g) kale or cabbage, thinly sliced | 3½oz (100g) green beans, trimmed and cut into 1in (2.5cm) pieces |

1

You want the onion to turn clear, not brown.

Ask an adult to heat the oil in a large saucepan and cook the onion and garlic over low heat for 3–4 minutes until soft.

2

Add the potato and carrots and cook the vegetables for 2–3 minutes.

3

Stir in the paprika, tomatoes, and stock. Ask an adult to bring it all to a boil before covering and simmering for 15 minutes.

4

Add the kale and green beans, then cook for another 6–7 minutes, or until tender. Season to taste and serve.

Ingredients

 1 tbsp sunflower oil **+**  1 onion, chopped **+** 1 garlic clove, chopped **+**  2 tsp finely grated ginger **+**

10 mins   30 mins   Serves 4

Squash & coconut curry

This yummy one-pot dish is packed with flavor. It's also just as good with sweet potato or pumpkin instead of squash.

Serve with rice and naan bread.

2 tbsp mild
curry powder

+

 1 large butternut
squash, peeled and cubed

+

 1 x 13.5fl oz (400ml)
can of coconut milk

+

 8oz (225g) green beans,
trimmed and chopped

1

Ask an adult to heat the oil in a large
frying pan over medium heat and cook
the onion, garlic, and ginger for 2–3 minutes.

2

Mix the curry powder
in and cook for 1 minute. It
will look like this once cooked.

3

See page 138
to learn how to
prepare squash.

Add the butternut squash
and 2 tbsp of water. Cook
for 1–2 minutes, until soft.

4

Pour the coconut milk and ¾ cup water on
top and carefully stir in the beans. An adult
should bring the mixture to a boil. Reduce the
heat, cover, and simmer for 15–20 minutes.

Ingredients

12oz (350g) dried
rigatoni or penne pasta

+

2 tbsp
olive oil

+

5½oz (150g) pancetta or
bacon, chopped

+

1 onion,
finely chopped

+

1 garlic clove,
crushed

Summer pasta

This simple pasta is a real breeze to make. The cherry tomatoes burst to help create the pasta sauce.

1

"Al dente" pasta is cooked but still a little firm.

Ask an adult to boil the pasta in lightly salted water for 8–10 minutes, until al dente.

2

Ask an adult to heat the oil in a large frying pan and add the pancetta, onion, and garlic. Cook for 4–5 minutes.

3

Carefully stir in the tomatoes, sugar, and red pepper flakes, if using. Ask an adult to cook for 5–6 minutes, stirring often, until the tomatoes start to burst.

1lb 2oz (500g)
cherry tomatoes

+

1 tsp sugar

+

Pinch of red pepper
flakes, optional

+

10 basil leaves,
thinly sliced

4

Ask an adult to drain the
pasta and reserve a little
of the cooking water. Add
the pasta and basil to the
pan and combine. If
the mix is too thick, stir
in a little pasta water.

Sprinkle
with grated
Parmesan
cheese.

Rigatoni pasta
is great for
holding sauce.

5 mins   21 mins   Serves 4

5 mins | 12 mins | Serves 4

Tomato soup

This soup is really fresh and easy. Best of all, it happens in a few minutes and in one pan. It's "soup-er simple!"

FRESH BASIL PAIRS WELL WITH TOMATOES.

Sprinkle with basil leaves and freshly ground black pepper. Serve with bread.

Ingredients

 + + + + + + + +

1 tbsp olive oil | 1 small onion, chopped | 1 garlic clove | 2 x 14oz (400g) cans peeled whole plum tomatoes | 2 tbsp tomato paste

1

You want the onion to turn soft but not brown.

Ask an adult to heat the oil in a pan and cook the onion and garlic on low heat for about 5 minutes.

2

Stir in the tomatoes, tomato paste, and sugar. Ask an adult to pour in the stock and bring to a boil, then reduce the heat and simmer for 5 minutes.

3

Ask an adult to use an immersion blender to blend the soup until smooth. Season to taste.

Ask an adult to open cans. The lid and inside rim are really sharp.

Canned tomatoes

Fresh tomatoes are only at their best for a short time each year, but good-quality canned versions allow us to have ripe tomatoes all year round.

Canned tomatoes come either whole or diced. You can also buy puree, which is blended tomatoes.

1 tsp sugar

+

1½ cups hot vegetable stock

Ingredients

1 large roasting chicken about 4½lb (2kg)

+

1 tbsp olive oil

+

2 onions, cut into quarters

+

2 celery ribs, trimmed and chopped

+

2 carrots, peeled and chopped

Roasted chicken

35 mins, plus 20 mins resting   2 hours   Serves 6

Roasting a chicken is simple and economical. Any leftovers you have can be used in other recipes in this book.

CRISPY SKIN

 + +

1 lemon, halved

Fresh herbs (thyme, rosemary, and bay), chopped

4¼ cups hot chicken stock

1 tbsp all-purpose flour

1

⚠ Ask an adult to preheat the oven to 425°F (220°C). Rub the chicken with the oil and season with salt and freshly ground black pepper.

Chicken tips

🐔 For best results, remove the chicken from the fridge 30 minutes before cooking. This will help the chicken to cook evenly.

🐔 Always thoroughly wash your hands with hot, soapy water after touching raw chicken.

2

Place the onions, celery, carrots, and chicken in a roasting pan. Squeeze the lemon on top and place in the cavity (inside the chicken) along with the herbs. Pour ¾ cup water into the roasting pan.

3

For the gravy, ask an adult to add the stock and flour to the pan. Stir to create the gravy.

⚠ Ask an adult to roast it for 15 minutes, then reduce the temperature to 350°F (180°C) and roast it for about 90 minutes. Remove the tray from the oven and let it rest for 20 minutes while making the gravy.

Chicken & mango salad

A fresh, healthy salad is a great way to use up leftover cooked chicken. This version comes with a zesty, fruity dressing.

10 mins   Serves 2

ZESTY DRESSING

1

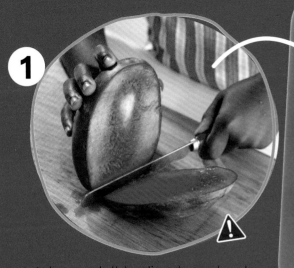
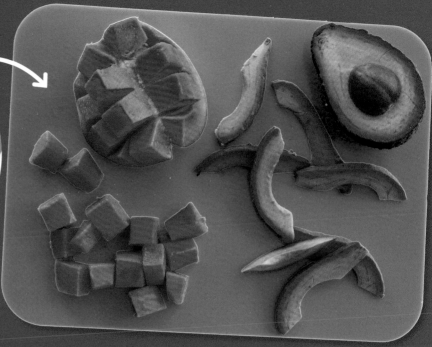

Ask an adult to slice two cheeks off the mango, avoiding the pit. Score squares into the flesh, then turn the cheeks inside out and scrape off the chunks. Ask an adult to halve the avocado, remove the pit, peel it, and then cut it into wedges.

2

In a small bowl, mix the dressing ingredients together. Place all the salad ingredients except the mixed leaves into a large bowl and pour the dressing on top. Combine and serve on a bed of mixed salad.

For the dressing
- Grated zest of 1 lime
- 2 tbsp lime juice
- 1 tbsp soy sauce
- 1 tbsp honey
- 2 tsp fresh root ginger, grated

Ingredients

 + + +  +  +

| 1 ripe mango | 1 ripe avocado | 1 cup cooked, shredded chicken | ¼ cucumber, seeded and sliced | 2 tbsp chopped cilantro | 3½oz (100g) mixed salad leaves |

Chicken noodle soup

This is another way to use up leftover chicken. You can add almost any vegetables you like, too.

When liquid is simmering it should bubble lightly.

1 Ask an adult to place the stock, spring onions, and soy sauce in a large pan and bring to a boil. Reduce the heat to a simmer.

2 Ask an adult to add the noodles and carrots and simmer for another 2 minutes.

3 Ask an adult to stir in the mangetout, corn, and chicken. Simmer for 3–4 minutes until the noodles and vegetables are tender. Serve immediately.

Ingredients

 +  + +

6½ cups hot chicken stock

4 spring onions, trimmed and sliced

1 tsp dark soy sauce

9oz (250g) dried egg noodles

COMFORTING AND HEALTHY!

1 carrot, peeled and cut into thin strips

4½oz (125g) snow peas, trimmed

1½ cups canned corn

1⅓ cups cooked, shredded chicken

Sweet treats and baked goods

Everybody likes a treat every now and then, and these savory bakes and sweet delights will always hit the spot.

Ingredients

| 2 lemons | 1½ cups self-rising flour | ½ tsp baking soda | ½ tsp salt | ½ cup granulated sugar |

Lemon muffins

These bright, zingy muffins are a real treat.
They're light and fluffy, but packed with flavor.

1

Ask an adult to preheat the oven to 375°F (190°C). Line a muffin pan with 8 muffin liners.

2

Dry ingredients

Grate the zest from one lemon into a bowl. Add the flour, baking soda, salt, sugar, and poppy seeds. Ask an adult to cut the lemon in half. Juice the halves into another bowl.

3

Wet ingredients

Beat the milk, egg, oil, and lemon juice in a bowl, then pour the wet ingredients into the dry. Stir until just combined.

4

Spoon into the liners and ask an adult to bake in the oven for 20–25 minutes until risen. Cool the muffins on a wire rack.

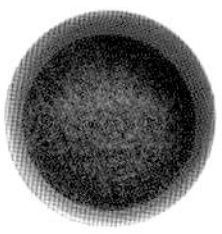

2 tbsp poppy seeds  + ¾ cup milk 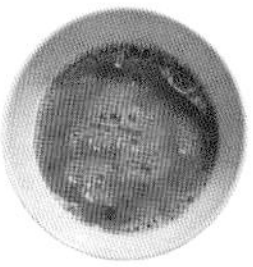 + 1 egg, beaten  + ⅓ cup sunflower oil

5

For the icing
- ⅔ cup confectioners' sugar
- 2 tsp grated lemon zest
- 2 tsp lemon juice

DECORATE WITH GRATED LEMON ZEST OR JELLIED LEMON SLICES.

Mix the ingredients for the icing in a small bowl. Drizzle the icing on the muffins once they are cool.

For this recipe, you will need eight muffin liners.

10 mins   25 mins   Makes 8

¾ cups plain yogurt

+

1 cup milk

+

1 tsp pure vanilla extract

+

¾ cup
old-fashioned oats

+

7oz (200g)
mixed berries

+

4 tbsp honey, maple
syrup, or nut butter

Overnight oats

Mix up this delicious breakfast a day before
and let the magic happen while you're sleeping.

Try out other
soft fruit, such
as sliced apricots,
peaches, or mango.

5 mins,
plus 6 hours or
overnight soaking

Serves 4

1

In a large bowl, mix together the yogurt, milk, and vanilla. Stir until the mixture is smooth.

2

Add the oats and stir well. Cover and place in the fridge to chill overnight or for at least 6 hours.

Use mixed berries of your choice, such as raspberries, blueberries, and strawberries.

3

The next day, loosen with a little water, if needed. Divide among the bowls and serve topped with fresh berries and a tablespoon of honey, maple syrup, or nut butter.

Ingredients

Olive oil, for greasing

+

2½ cups
rolled oats

+

1 cup almonds,
coarsely chopped

+

⅔ cup mixed seeds (sunflower,
pumpkin, and sesame)

+

Granola bars

These chunky treats are great for breakfast
or as a quick snack. The peanut butter and
dates make them really soft and chewy!

15 mins   25 mins   Makes 16

For this recipe,
you will need
an 11 x 7in
(28 x 18cm)
baking pan.

STORE ANY
LEFTOVER BARS
IN AN AIRTIGHT
CONTAINER.

½ cup honey

 ½ cup
peanut butter

 ¾ cup
pitted dates

¾ cup dried mixed berries (blueberries,
cherries, and cranberries) or raisins

1

Ask an adult to preheat the oven to
350°F (180°C). Lightly oil the baking pan
and add the oats, almonds, and seeds.
Ask an adult to bake it for 10–12 minutes.

2

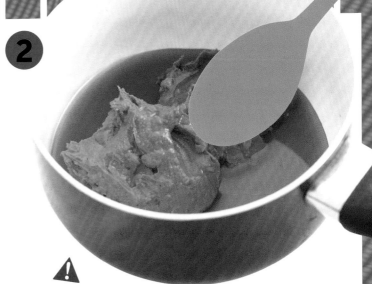

Ask an adult to warm the honey
and peanut butter in a pan over low
heat. Stir occasionally until combined.

3

Ask an adult to put the dates, ¼ cup of
warm water, and the honey mixture in a
food processor and blend until smooth.

4

*Allow to cool
slightly, then ask
an adult to cut into
bars and let set
in the pan.*

Combine the date mixture and the oat
mixture in a large bowl with the dried
berries or raisins. Spoon into a pan and
flatten with the back of a spoon. Ask
an adult to bake the mixture for 12 minutes.

Easiest flatbreads ever

These flatbreads are ready to eat in minutes. They are incredibly delicious brushed with garlic butter.

YOU CAN ALSO ADD PARSLEY TO THE MELTED BUTTER.

SPRINKLE WITH CHOPPED FLAT-LEAF PARSLEY.

 8 mins   4 mins each  Makes 12

Ingredients

 2½ cups all-purpose flour, plus extra for dusting **+** 1 tsp baking powder **+** ½ tsp salt **+** 1½ cups plain yogurt **+** 1 garlic clove, crushed **+** 3 tbsp butter, melted

1

Coarse dough

Place the flour, baking powder, salt, and yogurt in a bowl and mix together until coarsely combined.

2

Flour stops the dough from sticking.

Lightly dust a surface with flour, then knead the mixture for about 2 minutes to make a smooth dough.

3

⚠ Using a table knife, carefully cut the dough in half, then slice each half into 6 pieces. Roll the pieces into balls, then roll out on a floured surface until ⅛in (3mm) thick. Mix the garlic in the melted butter.

4

⚠ Ask an adult to place a grill pan over high heat and cook each flatbread for 1–2 minutes on both sides, until puffed up. Brush the flatbreads with the butter.

Focaccia

This dimpled Italian bread can be flavored with herbs, cheese, tomatoes, or olives. Follow this basic recipe or add your favorite ingredients.

BEST SERVED WARM,
DIPPED IN A SMALL
BOWL OF OLIVE OIL
WITH BALSAMIC VINEGAR.

15 mins, plus 2 hrs rising

25 mins

Serves 8

For this recipe, you will need an 11 x 7in (28 x 18cm) baking pan.

Ingredients

 + +  + +

¼ cup olive oil, plus extra for greasing + 2½ cups bread flour + 2 tsp dried yeast + 1 tsp salt + 1 cup lukewarm water

1

Lightly grease the pan with oil and set aside. Sift the flour into a large bowl and stir in the yeast and salt.

2

Make a well in the center and add the water and oil. Mix until it starts to come together and forms a smooth dough.

3

Knead on a clean surface for 10 minutes until smooth and elastic. Then cover in a clean bowl and let rise for 1 hour.

4

Press the dough into the pan so it fills all the corners. Cover with plastic wrap and let rise for an hour.

5

To finish
- 1 tbsp olive oil
- Sprigs of rosemary
- Sea salt, for sprinkling

DIMPLES

Ask an adult to preheat the oven to 400°F (200°C). Use your fingertips to make dimples over the bread and top with the oil, rosemary, and sea salt. Ask an adult to bake the bread for 20–25 minutes until golden and crispy.

Chocolate slab

What's better than chocolate? A slab of chocolate with nuts and berries. Shards of this slab make a great gift, if you can resist them yourself!

15 mins, plus 2 hrs chilling

10 mins

Serves 6–8

SNAP INTO LITTLE SHARDS.

CHOPPED PISTACHIO

For this recipe, you will need a 13 x 9in (33 x 23cm) baking pan.

Ingredients

Olive oil, for greasing

+

1lb 5oz (600g) milk chocolate, broken into pieces

+

7oz (200g) white chocolate, broken into pieces

+

Selection of chopped nuts, dried fruit, or freeze-dried raspberries

---

1

Lightly brush the baking pan with the oil, then line with baking paper.

2

Place the milk chocolate in a large heatproof bowl. Ask an adult to place the bowl over a pan of simmering water to melt the chocolate. Stir occasionally.

3

Ask an adult to pour the melted chocolate into the pan, tipping it from side to side to fill the corners.

4

Ask an adult to melt the white chocolate as before, then drizzle small amounts into the pan. Make swirly patterns with a toothpick.

5

Scatter with your desired toppings, then let set in the fridge for about 2 hours.

Make mini versions in a muffin pan.

Ingredients

12 tbsp unsalted butter
(1½ sticks), softened

+

⅔ cup
granulated sugar

+

3 medium
eggs, beaten

+

Grated zest
of 1 orange

+

1 tsp baking powder

+

1½ cups
self-rising flour

118

Orange cake

This easy sponge cake recipe is made by the all-in-one method, where all the ingredients are whisked together.

DECORATE WITH ORANGE ZEST.

For this recipe, you will need two 8in (20cm) cake pans.

SWEET FILLING

For the filling
- 5 tbsp unsalted butter, softened
- 1¾ cups confectioners' sugar, sifted
- 2 tbsp orange juice
- Grated zest of 1 orange

15 mins   30 mins   Serves 8

1

Ask an adult to preheat the oven to 350°F (180°C). Grease the cake pans and line the bottoms with parchment paper.

2

Place all the ingredients in a large bowl. Beat everything together using an electric hand mixer until well-mixed and thick.

3

Divide the mixture between the pans and level the tops. Ask an adult to bake the cakes in the oven for 25–30 minutes. Remove from the oven.

4

Let cool in the pans for 5 minutes. Ask an adult to turn the cakes onto wire racks to fully cool. Carefully remove the parchment paper from the bottoms.

5

To make the filling, mix the butter, confectioners' sugar, orange juice, and zest until creamy and smooth.

6

Spread half the filling on the bottom side of one of the cakes. Lay the other cake on top and spread the remaining filling over it.

Ingredients

7 tbsp butter, cut into cubes

+

2lb (900g) Granny Smith apples, peeled, cored, and sliced

+

½ cup dark brown sugar

+

2 tbsp apple juice

+

⏱ 10 mins 🕐 50 mins 🍴 Serves 6-8

Apple crumble

This classic dessert is as simple as it is delicious. The best thing about a crumble is the mix of crunchy topping and soft filling.

SERVE WITH EITHER ICE CREAM OR CUSTARD.

CRUNCHY TOPPING

¾ cup all-purpose flour

+

 1½ cups rolled jumbo oats

+

 ¼ cup mixed seeds, such as sunflower and pumpkin

+

 1 tsp ground cinnamon

1

The sugar will turn into a syrup when it cooks.

Ask an adult to preheat the oven to 350°F (180°C) and melt 2 tbsp of the butter in a pan. Stir in the apples, half the sugar, and the apple juice.

2

Ask an adult to cook the mixture for 5–6 minutes, covered, then spoon it into a 1-quart ovenproof dish.

3

Place the flour in a bowl and rub in the remaining butter with your fingertips until it looks like bread crumbs. Stir in the oats, remaining sugar, seeds, and cinnamon.

4

Spoon the mixture over the the apples. Ask an adult to bake the crumble for 30–40 minutes until the topping is golden.

Raspberry ice

This dessert is colorful, tasty, and refreshing. You can swap out the raspberries for other fruits if you like.

SPOON INTO SMALL GLASSES OR BOWLS.

SERVE WITH WAFERS.

Ingredients

 + **+** **+**

½ cup granulated sugar   ¾ cup cold water   1lb (450g) raspberries   2 tbsp lime juice

1

Ask an adult to bring the sugar and water to a boil, then reduce and simmer for 5 minutes until you have a syrup. Let cool.

2

Place the raspberries and lime juice in a food processor. Ask an adult to blend until you have a thick puree.

3

Add the mixture to a strainer over a bowl. Use a spoon to press the mixture through the strainer, then discard the seeds.

4

Pour the cooled syrup into the raspberry mixture, then pour into a shallow plastic container and freeze for 2 hours.

5

Remove from the freezer and carefully scrape with a fork, mixing the solid mixture into the liquid mixture.

6

Before serving, transfer to the fridge for 20 minutes to soften.

Return to the freezer and repeat the process twice at 30-minute intervals. Freeze a final time. Store in the freezer until ready to serve.

Ingredients

7 tbsp
butter, softened

½ cup
granulated sugar

1 egg

½ tsp pure vanilla
extract

1 cup
self-rising flour

124

Clever cookies

By adding a few different ingredients to this basic dough, you can have a variety of tasty treats. How clever is that?

WHITE CHOCOLATE AND CRANBERRY

BLUEBERRY AND LEMON

CINNAMON AND RAISIN

CHOCOLATE CHUNK

10 mins   15 mins   Makes 18

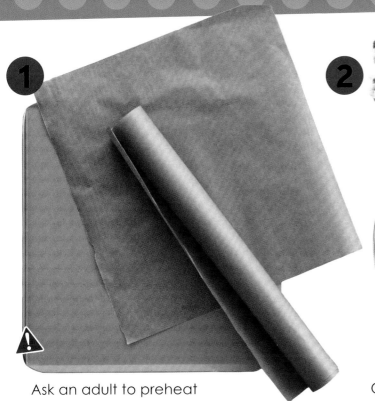

1 Ask an adult to preheat the oven to 350°F (180°C). Line two baking sheets with parchment paper.

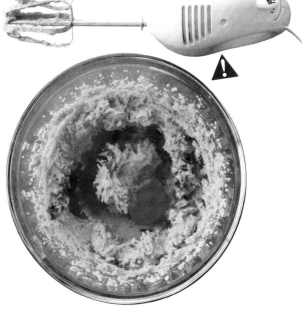

2 Cream the butter and sugar together with a hand mixer, then beat in the egg and vanilla extract.

3 Using a metal spoon, stir in the flour and any extra ingredients (see pages 126–127) and mix together.

4 Roll the dough into 18 balls and place on the baking sheets, leaving a little space around them. Flatten slightly and ask an adult to bake them for 12–15 minutes.

There are some great ingredient suggestions on the following pages.

Cinnamon & raisin

1 tsp ground cinnamon

¾ cup raisins

+

Chocolate chunks

2½oz (75g) dark chocolate chunks

2½oz (75g) white chocolate chunks

+

YOU CAN USE CHOCOLATE CHIPS IF YOU PREFER!

White chocolate & cranberry

½ cup
dried cranberries

+

3½oz (100g) white
chocolate chunks

Blueberry & lemon

2 tsp grated
lemon zest

+

3½oz (100g) fresh blueberries

Ingredients

1 x 11oz (320g) store-bought puff pastry sheet

+

1 egg, beaten

+

1 cup mascarpone

+

¾ cup heavy cream

+

2 tbsp confectioners' sugar, plus extra for decoration

+

2 tsp pure vanilla extract

128

Berry tart

This tasty tart is best when it's eaten on the day it's made, and since it's so delicious, there are unlikely to be any leftovers!

Try out other soft fruit, such as sliced apricots, peaches, or mango.

For the berry filling
- 4½oz (125g) strawberries, halved
- 4½oz (125g) blueberries
- 4½oz (125g) raspberries
- 4½oz (125g) cherries, pitted and halved

15 mins   20 mins   Serves 6

1

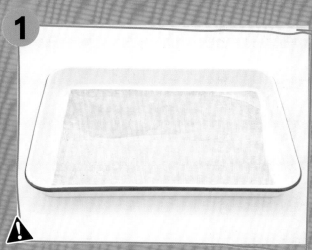

Ask an adult to preheat the oven to 400°F (200°C). Unroll the pastry sheet and place on a large nonstick baking sheet.

2

Ask an adult to use a sharp knife to score a 1in (2.5cm) rim along the sides of the rectangle, being careful not to cut all the way through. Prick the inside area lightly with a fork.

3

Brush the border with a little beaten egg. Ask an adult to cook the pastry in the center of the oven for 18–20 minutes, until it is risen and golden.

4

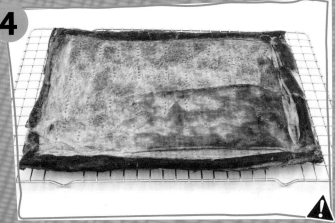

Ask an adult to carefully transfer the tart crust to a wire rack to cool completely.

5

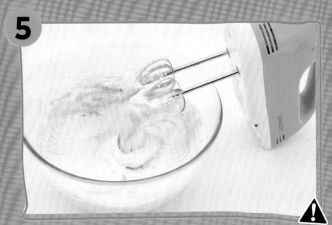

Beat the mascarpone cheese in a large bowl using a hand mixer until smooth. Add the heavy cream, confectioners' sugar, and vanilla, then beat until soft peaks form.

6

Fill the center of the tart with the cream mixture, keeping within the border. Top with the berries. Sprinkle with confectioners' sugar.

Ingredients

5 tbsp
unsalted butter

\+

1¾ cups crushed
graham crackers

\+

7oz (200g)
white chocolate

\+

1lb 2oz (500g)
mascarpone

\+

Cheesecake

This rich dessert is packed with
flavor and works just as well
with raspberries or strawberries.

20 mins, plus
30 mins chilling
15 mins
Serves 8

Crush the graham
crackers with
a rolling pin in a
plastic bag.

1

Ask an adult to melt the butter in
a pan and stir in the graham crackers.
Press into the base of the cake pan.

2

Ask an adult to melt the chocolate in
a bowl over a pan of simmering water,
stirring occasionally, until dissolved.

3

Beat until smooth.

Beat the mascarpone and confectioners'
sugar together with a hand mixer and
mix in the chocolate.

4

Smooth the mixture over the buttery
crust and chill for about 30 minutes,
until set.

3 tbsp confectioners' sugar, sifted

+

9oz (250g) fresh blackberries

+

¼ cup granulated sugar

+

1 tsp cornstarch

+

2 tsp lemon juice

5

Ask an adult to cook the blackberries and sugar in a saucepan over low heat for 2 minutes, stirring until the sugar dissolves.

6

Combine the cornstarch and lemon juice and ask an adult to add this to the blackberries. Cook for 2–3 minutes, then drizzle over the cheesecake.

For this recipe, you will need an 8in (20cm) loose-bottomed cake pan.

TOP WITH GRATED WHITE CHOCOLATE.

Chocolate mug brownies

These brownies are rich, gooey, and quick to make. Once you've made one for yourself, cook one for a friend.

SERVE WARM WITH A SCOOP OF ICE CREAM.

1 Mix the dry ingredients in a 7fl oz (200ml) microwavable cup or mug.

Ingredients

2 tbsp all-purpose flour

+

2 tbsp brown sugar

+

1 tbsp cocoa powder

+

Pinch of salt

2 Stir in the oil and milk until there are no lumps, then mix in the chocolate chunks or chips.

1 tbsp sunflower oil

+

2 tbsp milk

+

1 tbsp chocolate chunks or chips

3 Ask an adult to cook the brownie in a 1000w microwave on high for 1 minute. Let stand for 30 seconds.

133

Smoothies

Nothing beats a fruity smoothie on a hot day. Here are four quick recipes, but you can experiment and make your own, too.

Mango & banana

Flesh of 1 ripe mango

+

1 small banana, chopped

+

1¼ cups orange juice or coconut water

FULL OF FLAVOR!

Purple berry

1¼ cups apple juice

+

2½oz (75g) blueberries

+

2½oz (75g) blackberries

+

1 small banana, chopped

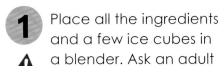 **1** Place all the ingredients and a few ice cubes in a blender. Ask an adult to blend until smooth.

2 Add a little more water, milk, or juice for the desired consistency.

3 Pour into glasses or chill in the fridge. Drink and enjoy!

Berry & vanilla

2¾oz (75g) strawberries, coarsely chopped + 2½oz (75g) raspberries

+ ½ cup vanilla yogurt + ½ cup milk

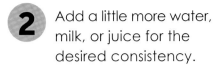

Super green

2 kiwis, peeled and chopped + 1 apple, cored, peeled, and chopped

Juice of 1 lime + ¾ cup cold water

+ 1¾oz (50g) spinach leaves

Kitchen terms

Don't worry if you come across a word in this book that you don't understand. These explanations will help you out.

Al dente
Pasta that is cooked through but still slightly firm when bitten.

Bake
Cooking food in an oven.

Beat
Stirring ingredients quickly using a hand mixer, whisk, or fork until they combine into a smooth mixture.

Blend
Mixing ingredients together in a blender or food processor until combined.

Boil
Cooking liquid in a pan over high temperature so that it bubbles strongly.

Broil
Cooking food from one direction at a time, usually using high heat.

Chill
Placing ingredients or a dish in the fridge to cool down or keep cool.

Combine
Mixing several ingredients together.

Chop
Using a knife to cut ingredients into smaller pieces.

Core
Removing the center of a piece of fruit to take out the seeds.

Cream
Quickly combining butter and sugar together to create a light, fluffy mixture.

Dice
Cutting an ingredient into small, equal cubes.

Drain
Removing excess liquid by pouring ingredients through a colander or strainer, or by resting on paper towels.

Drizzle
Pouring a small amount of liquid, such as olive oil or salad dressing, over a dish.

Fold
Using a spatula to gently mix ingredients together so that they stay light and fluffy.

Grate
Shredding an ingredient into little pieces by rubbing it against a grater.

Grease
Spreading a layer of butter or oil on a pan to stop ingredients from sticking to it.

Juice
Squeezing the liquid out of fruits or vegetables.

Knead
Working a dough by stretching and pulling until it becomes smooth and elastic.

Line
Placing parchment paper or foil in a pan so that food won't stick to it.

Marinate
Soaking ingredients in a flavorful liquid to add flavor.

Mash
Crushing ingredients with a fork or potato masher.

Mix
Combining ingredients together, either by hand or with equipment.

Pit
Remove the stone from fruit or vegetables.

Preheat
Turning the oven on 15 minutes before it is needed so that it reaches the recommended temperature before the food goes in.

Roll
Flattening out and shaping dough or pastry using a rolling pin.

Rub in
Rubbing flour and butter together with your fingers to create a texture that is similar to bread crumbs.

Score
Making shallow cuts across the surface of an ingredient.

Season
Adding salt, pepper, vinegar, or other spices to a dish to add flavor.

Set
Leaving food on the stove, counter, in the fridge, or in the freezer until it firms up and turns solid.

Sift
Using a strainer to remove lumps from dry ingredients, such as flour.

Simmer
Cooking a liquid over low heat so that it bubbles gently.

Slicing
Using a knife to cut food into strips.

Stir-fry
Cooking ingredients in a pan very quickly over high heat while stirring.

Strain
See "drain."

Whisk
Whipping up ingredients using a whisk. Used to introduce air into the mixture.

Useful skills

There are some cooking techniques that you'll use over and over again. Follow these steps to learn these skills and you'll be an expert in no time!

Cooking fluffy rice

The perfect rice is light and fluffy. This simple method works every time.

1. Measure out a ratio of 1 part rice to 1.5 parts cold water. Wash the rice under cold water until it runs clear, then add to a saucepan.

2. Ask an adult to bring to a boil, then cover and reduce to a simmer. Cook for 10 minutes, then turn off the heat and leave to steam, covered, for another 10 minutes.

Prepping squash

Squash makes for a healthy ingredient in many dishes. Here's a simple method for preparing it.

1. Place the squash on a cutting board. Ask an adult to cut it lengthwise in half.

2. Carefully scoop out the seeds from each half using a spoon.

3. Ask an adult to peel the squash and cut it into small cubes.

Prepping avocado

Avocado is a great addition to many dishes, but it can be tricky to get the pit out if you've never done it before.

1. Place the avocado on a cutting board and ask an adult to slice it lengthwise, all the way around, avoiding the pit.

2. Twist the avocado to separate it into two halves, then use a spoon to remove the pit.

3. Scoop out the flesh with a spoon and either ask an adult to slice it into pieces or carefully mash it with a fork yourself.

Rolling out pastry

Good quality store-bought dough is a great time-saver. All you need to do is roll it out.

1 Sprinkle flour onto a rolling pin and your work surface. Use the rolling pin to push down and forward over the dough, using long, steady strokes.

2 Turn the dough around and repeat as necessary, until it reaches your desired thickness.

Separating eggs

Some recipes only require the egg white or yolk. Luckily, it's easy to separate them.

1 Crack an egg on the side of a bowl. Transfer the yolk back and forth from one half of the shell to the other, letting the white fall into the bowl and holding the yolk in the shell.

Shredding chicken

Shredded, leftover chicken can be used in lots of other dishes. It's a great way to get the most out of your ingredients.

1 Wait for the cooked chicken to cool thoroughly. Use one fork to hold it still and another to carefully pull it apart. Alternatively, ask an adult to slice the breasts off the carcass and pulse them in a food processor.

Dicing onions

Onions are used in lots of recipes, so learning how to dice one is a skill worth knowing.

1 Ask an adult to peel the onion and slice it in half from root to stem.

2 An adult should then make several vertical slices toward the root, being careful not to cut all the way to the end.

3 Ask an adult to repeat with horizontal cuts, then hold the onion together and slice down across the cuts you made earlier.

Lining a cake pan

Lining a pan will stop your cake from sticking to it, making it easier to remove.

1 Grease the pan by spreading a layer of oil or butter onto the bottom and sides.

2 Place the pan on the parchment paper and draw around the edges, leaving extra on all sides.

3 Ask an adult to cut the paper out. Press it into the pan, fold at the corners, and snip off any excess paper.

Kneading dough

Kneading dough can be quite a physical job, but at least it will make you strong!

1 Place the dough onto a floured surface. Using clean hands, stretch the dough by pushing it down and away from you with the heel of your hands.

2 Fold the dough back toward you. Rotate and repeat for 5–10 minutes until the dough has become smooth and elastic.

139

Weights and measurements

All the quantities for ingredients you'll need in this book are written right on the page, but this chart will be handy as you grow as a cook.

A guide to measurements

The type of measurements you use depends on the country you live in. We've listed both types here so that if you want to adjust the recipes in this book, or any others you find, you'll have this helpful chart.

Weights

¼oz	(10g)	5½oz	(150g)	1¾lb	(800g)
½oz	(15g)	6oz	(175g)	2lb	(900g)
¾oz	(20g)	7oz	(200g)	2¼lb	(1kg)
scant 1oz	(25g)	8oz	(225g)	2½lb	(1.1kg)
1oz	(30g)	9oz	(250g)	2¾lb	(1.25kg)
1½oz	(45g)	10oz	(300g)	3lb	(1.35kg)
1¾oz	(50g)	12oz	(350g)	3lb 3oz	(1.5kg)
2oz	(60g)	14oz	(400g)	4lb	(1.8kg)
2½oz	(75g)	1lb	(450g)	4½lb	(2kg)
3oz	(85g)	1lb 2oz	(500g)	5lb	(2.25kg)
3½oz	(100g)	1¼lb	(550g)	5½lb	(2.5kg)
4oz	(115g)	1lb 5oz	(600g)	6lb	(2.7kg)
4½oz	(125g)	1½lb	(675g)	6½lb	(3kg)
5oz	(140g)	1lb 10oz	(750g)		

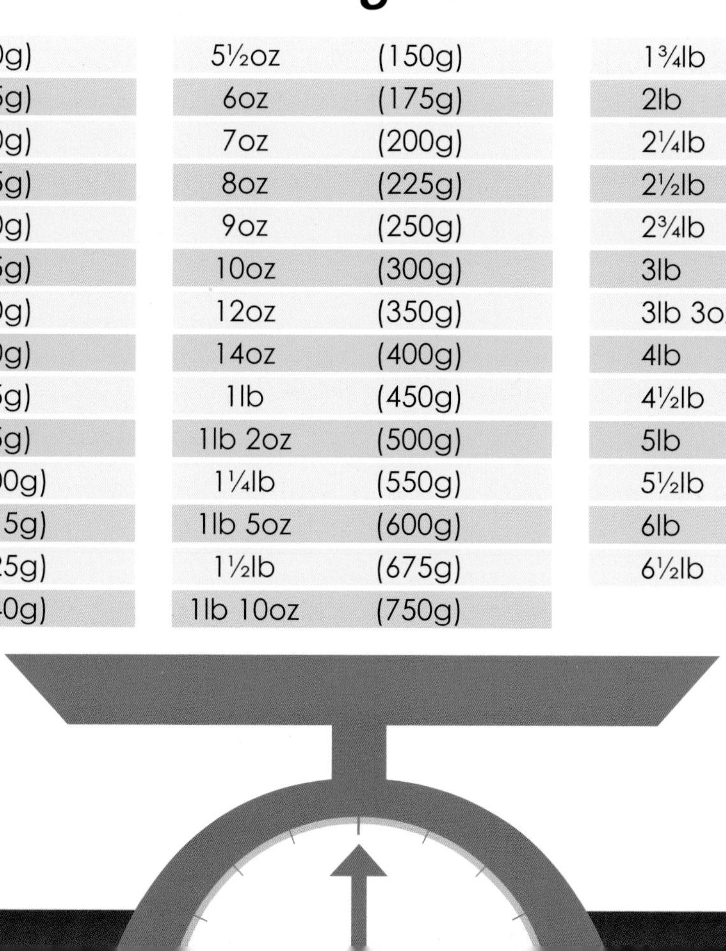

Volume measurements

3 tsp   =   1 tbsp

2fl oz	(4 tbsp)	7fl oz	(200ml)	15fl oz	(450ml)
2½fl oz	(75ml)	8fl oz	(240ml)	16fl oz	(500ml)
3fl oz	(90ml)	9fl oz	(250ml)	20fl oz	(600ml)
3½fl oz	(100ml)	10fl oz	(300ml)	25fl oz	(750ml)
4fl oz	(120ml)	12fl oz	(350ml)	30fl oz	(900ml)
5fl oz	(150ml)	14fl oz	(400ml)	35fl oz	(1 liter)

Oven temperatures

(250°F)	130°C
(275°F)	140°C
(300°F)	150°C
(325°F)	160°C
(350°F)	180°C
(375°F)	190°C
(400°F)	200°C
(425°F)	220°C
(450°F)	230°C
(475°F)	240°C

Index

Acknowledgments

The publisher would like to thank the following for their kind permission to reproduce their photographs:

(Key: a-above; b-below/bottom; c-center; f-far; l-left; r-right; t-top)

6–7 Dreamstime.com: Liubirong. **8–9 Dreamstime.com:** Liubirong. **10 Dreamstime.com:** Konstantin Kirillov / Kvkirillov (crb). **11 123RF.com:** Zoran Mladenovic/feelphotoart (tc). **Dreamstime.com:** Afe207 (tc/Bamboo mat). **19 Dreamstime.com:** Chernetskaya (br). **22 Dreamstime.com:** Nedim Bajramovic (tl/rice); Daniel Rnneberg (tc). **23 Dreamstime.com:** Chernetskaya (tr/wasabi); Dzmitry Shpak (tl/seaweed); Nina Moskovchenko (tc/ginger); Nuttanin Kanakornboonyawat (tl). **27 Dreamstime.com:** Baibaz (br). **34 Dreamstime.com:** Reinis Bigacs (cla); Kewuwu (tl); Anton Starikov (cla/rice paper); Natalia Zakharova (cl). **48 Dreamstime.com:** Chernetskaya (tl); Ricky Soni Creations (tr/chilli powder). **56 Dreamstime.com:** Chernetskaya (bl). **60 Dreamstime.com:** Baibaz (cl). **66 Dreamstime.com:** Katyenka (tl/curry). **67 Dreamstime.com:** Jiri Hera (tr/bamboo). **74 Dreamstime.com:** Liudmyla Chuhunova (tr/beans). **75 Dreamstime.com:** Chernetskaya (tr/lemon); Funandrejs (tl/pesto). **77 Dreamstime.com:** Baibaz (tc/oil). **89 Dreamstime.com:** Peter Hermes Furian (tl/rosemary); Yulia Gusterina (tl/risotto). **92 Dreamstime.com:** Chernetskaya (tl). **107 Dreamstime.com:** Chernetskaya (tr). **128 Depositphotos Inc:** belchonock (tl). **133 Dreamstime.com:** Chernetskaya (clb/oil). **136–137 Dreamstime.com:** Liubirong. **140–141 Dreamstime.com:** Liubirong. **142–143 Dreamstime.com:** Liubirong. **144 Dreamstime.com:** Liubirong.

Cover images: *Front:* **Dreamstime.com:** Alison Gibson (texture); *Back:* **Dreamstime.com:** Alison Gibson tl/(texture); *Spine:* **Dreamstime.com:** Alison Gibson t

All other images © Dorling Kindersley Limited

THIS EDITION

DK would like to thank Helen Peters for indexing, Dawn Henderson for proofreading, Anne Damerell for legal assistance, Radhika Haswani and Pranay Mathur for editorial support, and Anna Bonnerjea, Francesca Harper, and Jessica Tapolcai for helping at the photoshoots.

PREVIOUS EDITION

DK would like to thank James Tye for additional photography, Marie Lorimer for indexing, Eleanor Bates, Lynne Murray, Sakshi Saluja, and Romaine Werblow for picture library assistance, and Rachael Hare, Violet Peto, and Artie King for help during the photoshoots.